SO WHERE DO WE GO NOW?

Jason Zuniga

TABLE OF CONTENTS

forgive & forget

sinking

Evaluate

grieve

fear

discreet

hate

Cope

Question

Phases

looking at you

23

trains

high expectations

Clothes off

Come to grips

the apology letter

getting better

Peace of mind

Checking In

priviliges

i love you

RECOVER

Gifted

not yet

thank you for saving me

because of you

to take away

line in the sand

You'll see

pressure

Real Gains

spill

stop

Listen!

progress

Patience

white out

scream

zipper

come back

A thought

Feeling feelings

turn back

Driving

breathe

Still breathing

it's familiar

Lonely

processing

Damaged goods

Karma

stay

Not my valentine

Not going to

choosing

To lose

growth

HEALING   **140**

Comfort

moment

still alive

instruction

roses

feels like home

the truth

Time

Grieving

the start and the finish

you don't understand

You still get to me

every thirty minutes

I guess some things, I'll never know

Will you catch me?

Believing in myself

Accepting choices

Just wanted to tell you

Labels

Not anymore

This candle

Grateful

When i think of you

What's Left

Goodbye

The end

I could be lonely

monsters

Letting go

Love yourself

so, where do we go now

Thank you

BASELINE

FOR ME

Jason,

There's a load of life lessons down the way from where you stand,

All with your name on them.

Don't be afraid.

Eventually, you live and you learn.

Life has a lot of cruel ways to tell you to stay strong.

Pain is its gift, and it came with love.

And it's worth every tear from your eyes.

You won't know it, then,

And that's okay.

Love, loss, heartbreak, sacrifice, struggle—everything that's ever going

to make you question whether or not this world deserves your footsteps—

Is worth feeling every bit of.

Don't be afraid of being lost.

I'm still searching for an answer to the questions,

But never question the love that you carry,

For anyone,

And especially for yourself.

STEPPING STONE

A free soul that stays complacent,
Standing on the same placement.
Hands on till I'm replaced and
Left behind in the basement.

Just a stepping stone,
Watching others stepping stoned.
I'm here to catch your one step back,
And push you till you're stepping home.

A moment, a good time, maybe even a friend.
A brother, a son, maybe a girl's boyfriend.
A mistake, a disappointment, a hero that I pretend.
A stepping stone, a closure, a chapter's "The End."

DISGUISE

Do I look the part?
At least I can dress like I got it figured out.
I've convinced you that much.
Let's see how far this goes.

GROWING UP

I found comfort in isolation.

I found understanding in TV screens and comic books.

I found joy in stick figures I drew on pieces of paper.

I found love in my mother's arms.

It was all so simple.

It didn't take much to keep me entertained.

And bad days were nothing more than just bad days.

Mental health was unheard of.

I was happier to not know shit.

Nowadays, I find comfort in isolation.

I find understanding in screens and comic books.

I find joy in creating anything that comes to mind.

And I find love in the arms of warm hearts.

It's a lot more complex now.

I find entertainment in the little things.

I don't have bad days anymore

I have bad moments.

Mental health is a huge aspect in my life.

I really was happier in not knowing shit.

MAY NOT

I may not be the easiest to love,
But I'll love easily.
I may make it hard for people to stay around,
But I'll stay around as long as you need.
I may not be the first choice,
But I've accepted the safe option.
And I may not be afraid to die,
But I'm afraid of losing you.

THE DIFFERENCE

Pushing to save them,
Pulling to save me.

Pushing to protect me,
Pulling to save me.

CONNECT

If I try to connect,
What's inside, I'll forget.
Every trial in my debt,
Covered smiles, with regret.
Colored tiles in my steps,
Every mile is a test.
Been a while since I left
All the piles of neglect.

AFRAID

I'm not afraid to die.

I'm afraid of living.

I'm not afraid of the ending.

I'm afraid of what I'll go through before I get there.

~~I feel like my~~ I feel in a rut.
I feel more than my enemy does.
I feel less than a buzz.
More than a tingling fuzz.
My body is numb.
im rotting from what I've become.
Been falling in love.
But stalling in all of the things that I want.
Never thought I would fall. this hard.
I'm scared that one day, it ~~would~~ fall apart.
                            will.

11

WHAT DO YOU WANT

I want a lit candle.

I want a warm blanket.

I want a picture of the sun.

I want a rose that never dies.

I want a love that never leaves.

I want a smile to wake up next to.

I want a song that heals my anxiety.

I want a sunset that reminds me of you.

I want a grief that reminds me to always love.

I want a mirror that shows me what I want to see.

I want a movie about my life with a happy ending.

I want a breath that takes away my heavy thoughts.

I want a heart that looks at mine and fills in the piece it's missing.

YOU

You swung into my life at a young age.

You taught me how to be tall, how to be brave.

You've shown me that it's possible 'cuz it's all in my brain.

You made me learn to love and respect my own name.

You taught me that a cape doesn't mean you're saved.

You were always there when I didn't feel safe.

You taught me how to appreciate the weather when it rained.

You are my role model 'cuz no one could claim.

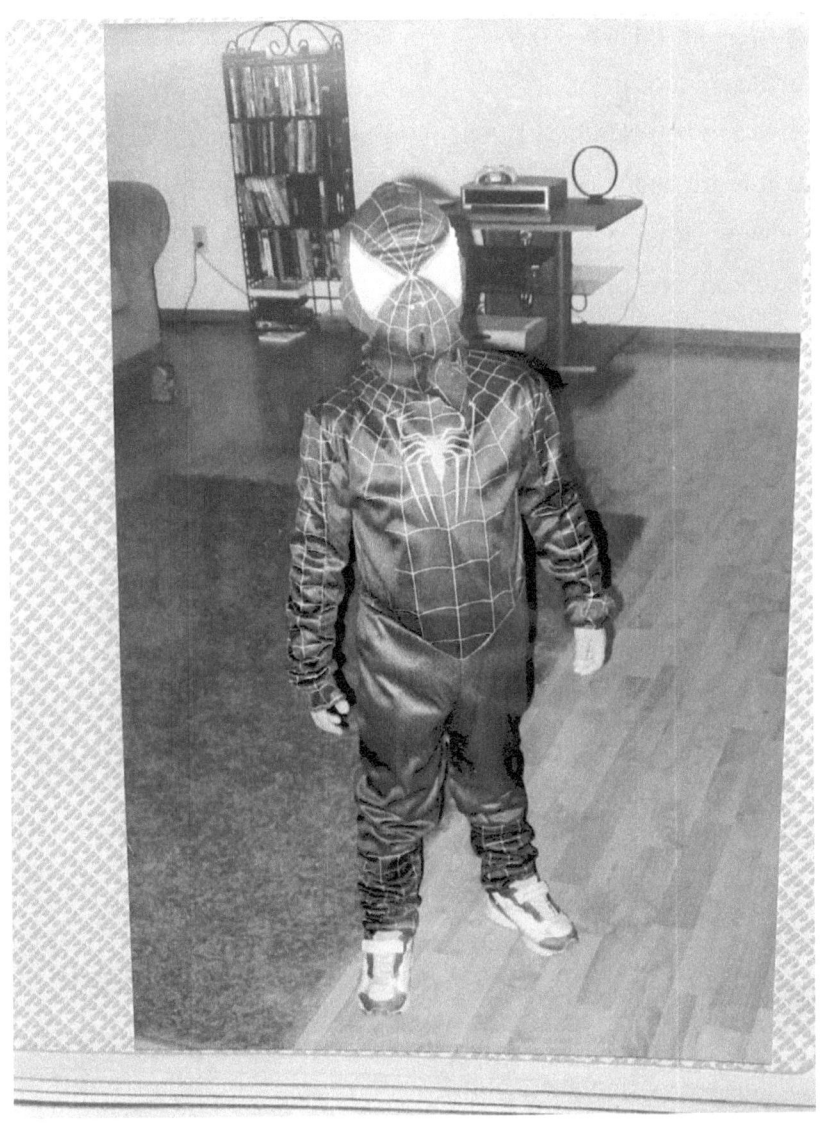

ANGELS

There's a special scar I wear.
It carries a lot of grief.
I learned to be grateful for the emotions it gives me,
'Cuz it reminds me of these two angels I knew.
They were so young and beautiful.
I got to hold one of them in my arms.
I was too young to understand at the time,
But if I had one wish,
I would want that moment back.
So I could embrace that moment,
For as long as I could.
'Cuz now, all I remember is a picture.
I didn't realize my first hello to them
Was also going to be my last goodbye.

I don't visit them as often anymore,
But every time I do, I cry.
For a while, those tears hurt,
'Cuz they fell down my face.

For faces I didn't get the chance to know.
Now, those tears make me smile.
'Cuz I get the chance to feel the love,
That I never got to give them,
That I get to carry for them till then.

HARSH

It'll never last long enough.

It'll never feel to its fullest.

Till next time.

BLIND

I have allowed you to be the storm over my comfort.

The voice that whispers only criticism that is five years old,

Yet, still the freshest cut on my skin.

The home in my mind has always left a room for you,

Because I struggle with saying no.

Especially to you.

Was that out of love or fear?

Somewhere down the way, I lost sight of where that line stood.

It's like I was blindfolded my whole life,

And your voice was my only guidance through this world that felt so massive to a sacred soul.

SPIRAL

These moments come and go.
I've thought about my last breath.
It's lonely.
Like, holding hands with my guilt—
So, deserving when the only other heartbeat around
Is in the mirror, sharing the same tragedy.
We both gave our hearts to everyone with an open hand.
So many people, carrying around a piece of my heart—
I lose track of them sometimes.
They disappear without a thank you.
Was it worth all the handouts
To be left with your hands out?
She's in my mind.
She'd be my last thought.
I don't believe in happy endings.
I'd be more heartbroken if I did—
Believing in the things you want the most in your conclusion,
Only to lie there, with a handful of memories
In the palm of your mind,
With nothing but tears to show for it.

It's sad.
To trust,
To have faith in someone to catch you when you fall
Every single time.

It's as terrifying as the concussion from the ground.
Would I be delusional enough to get back up
And fall again,
With nothing but recycled faith?
I don't believe in happy endings.
But I still would…

FIVE THINGS

I was told to write down five things that are important to me.
I missed the part where myself was supposed to be, at the top.
It was so easy for me to put down everything and everyone else.
Didn't realize I didn't even make the list.

HIGH-FUNCTIONING

I woke up.
Two hours later, I get out of bed.
I shower, brush my teeth, and put on a good fit.
Go to work.
Smile and laugh with you.
Tell you about my day, and hopefully do my job.
Enough to make a difference.

It's easy to hide.
I don't show symptoms.
I look just like you.
Like I have it all figured out.
I smile just like I do.
Laugh just like I do.

But when I close the door behind me,
I remind myself of the next thirty minutes.

ANOTHER BRANCH

I would stay in this moment forever.
I would replay it to relive it again.
I would watch it from the start to the end.
Like a script, down to the last letter.

A moment that life is worth to sever.
I cherish it, like it's my only friend.
A lot of these moments came and went.
An extra tight grip would hopefully keep us together.

But this isn't real life,
It's merely a thought.
Just another branch,

Created in my mind.
'Cuz it's all that I want,
Just another branch.

MY VOICE

My biggest critic.

My hardest judgment.

My closest friend.

You hold me accountable to my every choice.

You never let me hear the end of my mistakes.

Yet, I still found comfort in your words.

It's confusing.

I'm learning to find comfort in the words I should believe in.

Knowing and being more self-aware of what and when I should listen to those voices.

My voice.

DON'T

I don't think you heard me, when your back was turned.
I don't think you heard me, when I was trying to explain.
I don't think you heard me, when you were yelling over me.
I don't think you heard me, when I wasn't okay.

Maybe, I could've done more for your approval.
Maybe, I wouldn't have stayed quiet if I didn't feel silenced.
Maybe, I should've tried harder in your eyes.

I don't want to be like you.
I don't want to be who you want me to be.

I'm sorry for disappointing you.

PINNED

I remember when I was forced to be a part of you.
I was scared.
But then we clicked after some time.
I became comfortable around you.
I wanted more time with you.
I wanted to learn everything about you.
Yea, we had our ups and downs.
But who doesn't?
It wasn't love at first sight.
But it grew to feel like true love.

Eventually, it got toxic.
Family got involved between us.
After some time, it made it really hard to see the "why" in why I stuck
around for so long.
It made me confront, not only the people involved,
But myself, and everything I was holding inside about the situation.
Being honest for once,
Nowhere to hide myself and my feelings.

It was hard.
But nothing good ever came easy.
I decided to stick around for one more year.
But I didn't do it for everyone involved;
I did it for myself
And I was going to enjoy every moment of it,
That was the ultimate goal.
And I did.
I left with no regrets,
And I can now reflect on the 13 years I spent, enjoying the memories.

GRIEF

I carry in my pocket,

With my keys and wallet,

A necessity,

A piece of who I am.

I missed the part where you can't spare without it.

Worn like a ghost with a weighted blanket.

You either learn to carry the weight

Or learn to live with the weight.

The difference is who you become.

SPILLED MILK

Maybe it's the clouds, crying over my window.

Maybe it's the storm inside my chest.

Maybe it's the sleep that didn't feel like rest.

Maybe it's the threads—they've attached to my heart.

All I know is, there's a mess on the floor when I woke up,

And I've been crying over it for some time now.

I've tried cleaning it up,

But it seeps through everything I use to pick it up.

My voice has been trying to find its way out for help.

I think it got lost somewhere in the fog.

I could hear it from deep down.

I'm scared of losing it.

A MUSE

I took a big step the other day.
Maybe I'm trying to run away.
From the stains and messes I made,
On the floors that I don't lay on.
This is not my home.
This is not my choice.
I chose to be alone,
When you took away my voice.
You gave a hand to hold,
To let go of all the noise.
Now, you're gripping on my throat,
And speaking for things that I destroy.
You're scary to look at.
You're harder to look past.
The things that I would crash,
I rid, and you took back.
The thoughts that I would mask,
You told me they would last.
Now, I can't help but look sad,
At masks I used as…

THE PROBLEM

I've picked up the blame quicker than the last slice.
Never given the chance to be shared.
Never wanted that for anyone.
Guilt is like stains on a shirt.
I wear it everywhere.

HABITS

Biting the skin off my cheeks,
Biting until my lips bleed.
My anxiety triggers my teeth,
My anxiety tells me I need.

I NEED A HUG

I wish I could warn you ahead of time.
Tell you not to make this mistake.
We've made similar mistakes before, but this one…
This one takes the cake.

This one hurt, especially.
I thought, once the hard part was over,
I'd be at peace, finally.
But I'm not.

If anything, I'm so much more angry.
This anger has no escape.

Our words meant nothing to them.
Nothing changed that.
We tried.

We tried so hard.

I'LL BE FINE

If it makes you shine,
I'll carry this burden for you.
Don't worry, I'll be fine.

I'll never question why,
It's what I'm accustomed to.
If it makes you shine,

I'll give you all my time.
I'll pay out all your dues.
Don't worry, I'll be fine.

You may have crossed the line,
A little more than a few.
If it makes you shine,

I'll put my problems to the side.
There's no other option to choose.
Don't worry, I'll be fine.

I'll give you all of mine,
Every time I win or lose.
If it makes you shine,
Don't worry, I'll be fine.

SHOWER THOUGHTS

I wake up like everybody else does,
But I don't want to be like everybody else.
I put myself under everybody else 'cuz,
I'm no good at asking for anybody's help.

I know where I haven't been lately,
But I don't know where I am right now.
That small slice of hope for anyone to save me,
Is stronger than the promise that I vowed.

My biggest flaw is preparing for the worst,
My biggest strength is preparing, for the worst.
Being young is seeing the similarities,
Growing up is understanding the difference.

SPACED OUT

Our conversation reminded me of a moment,
I remembered,
I relived,
And I stayed in it,
It felt real again.

You didn't have to tap on my shoulder,
I was enjoying the moment.

PLAYING PRETEND

Playing pretend was my favorite game as a kid.

So much so, it's becoming my form of living.

Pretending I have the answers to your questions.

Pretending I'm stable enough to believe in my own advice.

I've never been much of a liar.

Or maybe that's been a long game on myself.

LOVE HURTS

Love hurts.

Yet, I can only love you more.

No matter how much it cuts me,

The stains end up on your shirt.

My blood never touches the ground.

You leave a seed in every wound.

I only grow after every cut.

We only get closer after every hurt.

We only smile more.

We only love more.

I'll hurt for you,

Every single time.

HURT AGAIN

If the imaginary string is connected to you,

Does that mean you'll carry everything I'm missing?
On my worst days, are you what takes the edge off?
Now that I'm here, is the time right?
Those questions burn my skin.

Where my heart sees that X-shaped hole,
All my secrets make you my journal.
Need is now thinking for you and I,
Thoughts of you need reassurance.

Tying me down feels like a dream,
One that I'm scared I'll wake up from.

Haven't had the best luck with love.
Underneath these layers is delicate.
Rocks with familiar faces made cracks.
Thrown at my shell, till I show weakness.

Another way of saying that I'm scared,
Giving myself to someone is having faith.
And faith is a very rare gem to come by,
I worry that this will look like a familiar chapter,
Never again.

TO TOMORROW

I'll take your hand and show you tomorrow,

I'll love you like my love never went borrowed.

Every tear, every drop of my sorrow,

Won't matter once we see tomorrow.

TO FALL

I learned to fall in love by jumping off the idea of denial.
Trusting that I would land in your arms with a smile.
Giving myself to someone has been scary for a while.
Being afraid of falling for an idea of someone,
Then feeling the impact from the tile.

Some would be willing to get back up to the next tempt,
But I'm still stopping the blood from my last attempt.
Gathering my thoughts, 'cuz some of them got swept
Under the rug and forgotten, the moment I left.

Now I'm here, not feeling my life pulled from inside,
But feeling you bring the life into me, up to my eyes.
If this is a ruse that guides me to my own demise,
I'm willing to die on this hill with love to be realized.

I LOVE YOU

Infinite different ways to say it.

Lying next to you in bed.
Obsessing over you when I get the chance.
Visualizing our future.
Exploring everything that makes you…

You
Over the moon and back, once more.
Universally enlightened by you.

MUTUALLY IN FREQUENCY

I've felt you in the darkness,

I didn't need light to see you're beautiful.

It's a feeling,

Like hands wiping away tears.

There's a sense of comfort in your skin,

I hold you to feel grounded.

To be reminded, we're safe,

Mutually in frequency,

And handled with care.

THE INTRO

I saw sparks.

Light inside of my heart.

The parts that were dark.

I chose to keep a part.

That was the start.

US?

Can it be just the "me and you?"
Do all the things we want to do?
This lonely road is meant for two,
And I believe that we're the perfect few.
Just me and you, and you and me,
You're the image that I choose to be.
You carry answers to the things I think.
Wisdom, poison, we're the fuel we drink.

BY CHOICE & WITH TIME

I've told you, I'm an open book.

And you've read almost every chapter,

By choice and with time.

I've shown you my stains and imperfections,

And you held me tighter,

By choice and with time.

I've shown you the labels I've been given,

And you said, "I don't judge a book by its cover."

By choice and with time.

And as I continue to write out my story,

You're by my side to fill the void,

By choice and with time.

INVESTING

I'll hold you through the hard times.

Kiss you on the rainy nights.

Share with you my life.

And hear every word that makes you inhale once more.

If life makes it harder for you to walk through,

I'll carry you until you regain your strength.

I'll do whatever it takes,

To remind you that love is an investment.

I'll spend all my time on.

JUST BREATHE

After I started to control my breath,
Not a sound was heard.
Xiphoid pains in my chest faded.
I felt feeling in my hands again,
Embracing what was in front of me.
Through all the fear, blinding my vision,
Your eyes were found in front of me.

WHO ARE YOU

You are the best part of me.
A mirror that makes me smile every time.
The sun, I'll always give roses to.
The silence that clouds over the loudest traffic in my head.
You are the missing piece to a puzzle that I've left unsolved for so long,
The heart-shaped piece, I only wish to nurture and cherish.

You are the love that tastes like homemade joy.
That love that feels like a never-ending hug made from your arms.
Love that smells like home away from home.
Love that has taught me what real love is supposed to feel like.
Real love.

But most of all,
You are a moment in time I want to live in for as long as time is willing
to give me.
A moment of my life that is worth every tear I've shed, to have you be
the one to wipe them off my face.
And the hardest part about it, which I'm still learning to tread through, is

Accepting that there is going to be a moment after you—
Where the clouds are going to pour over my head, and the fog will
cloud my vision until
You won't be there anymore.
Then the raindrops will be tears,
Tears that you won't wipe away.

You are my best friend.

THE TRANSITION

A blanket of snow, outside of my window.

A blanket of warmth, covering my legs.

The cold air, overwhelming uncovered skin.

The warm heater, protecting my home.

Winter is the most beautiful pain

So pleasing to the eye,

So uncomfortable to live in.

Someday, the white will change to green.

Vibrant textures will follow.

The outside world will come back to life,

And my seasonal depression will melt away with the snow.

Until then, I'm enjoying the view from inside.

And taking it, one day at a time.

CRISIS

STILL

Giving your best,
To continuously feel like it's
Not enough.

Is like saving your tears,
To put out a fire
That'll never go out.

TRYING

I gave you the best explanation that I can.

But what's the point when it's aiming at who I am?

Both reasons and excuses go together, holding hands.

It's hard when we both feel like we're being the bigger person.

youre kidding

you are one of the most
emotionally unstable
people I've ever met

I did absolutely nothing
wrong for you to treat me
like that but you know
what fuck you

congrats push everyone
away because you feel
like you're better than
everyone would truly
you're not

FAILURE

I've been lifted into the spotlight,
Only to break beneath it.
Now feeling the ground, covered in my shame,
While the void wallows in pity.
I'm hurting, but that's not the focus.
It's knowing that somewhere in that void,
Outside of the light,
Are people who counted on me.

I start to question myself and my strength.
Did I give everything I had,
What would've been enough?

It's like time stopped.
Just for me to live in this moment.
And feel it, long enough,
To pack it in and carry with me,
Till I learn to eventually let go.

REMIND ME

I remember when I fucked up that one time.
Thank you for reminding me of that one time.
I needed a reminder of how stupid I can be.
It's not like I wasn't telling myself off about the same thing.
I try to forgive myself and do better.
But I'm not perfect, and you tell me whenever.

I'm trying my best to do right,
You only see what I did wrong.
I do my best to try to fight,
The negative thoughts that go on.
I've been running out of light,
While the voices whistle along.
Been contemplating I just might
Join in singing the same song.

HEAR ME

The sound wasn't heard by an ear,
But it was enough to lose my voice.
It was enough to get the message across.
If only you heard me the first time.
Maybe things would've been different.
Maybe I wouldn't have this idea of myself.
Maybe I wouldn't have left.

DESERVED

Don't think I don't regret it,

Even with no expression.

Still, I know it's my fault,

Earning those words you said.

Reminding me of my mistakes,

Venting to the problem.

Ending my story,

Dotting my final "i."

ENOUGH

Love isn't enough to heal the wounds you inflicted,
Pain will always be remembered through the bliss.
It's not enough to say "I love you,"
You still did what you did.

THE PUPIL

I looked into the pupil under the bridge,
It was never-ending.
The moon couldn't find where it ends,
I stood over it with my last chance in both grips of my hands.
Asking myself, "What's your reason?"
Staring down, while it stares back at me,
Waiting for my choice.

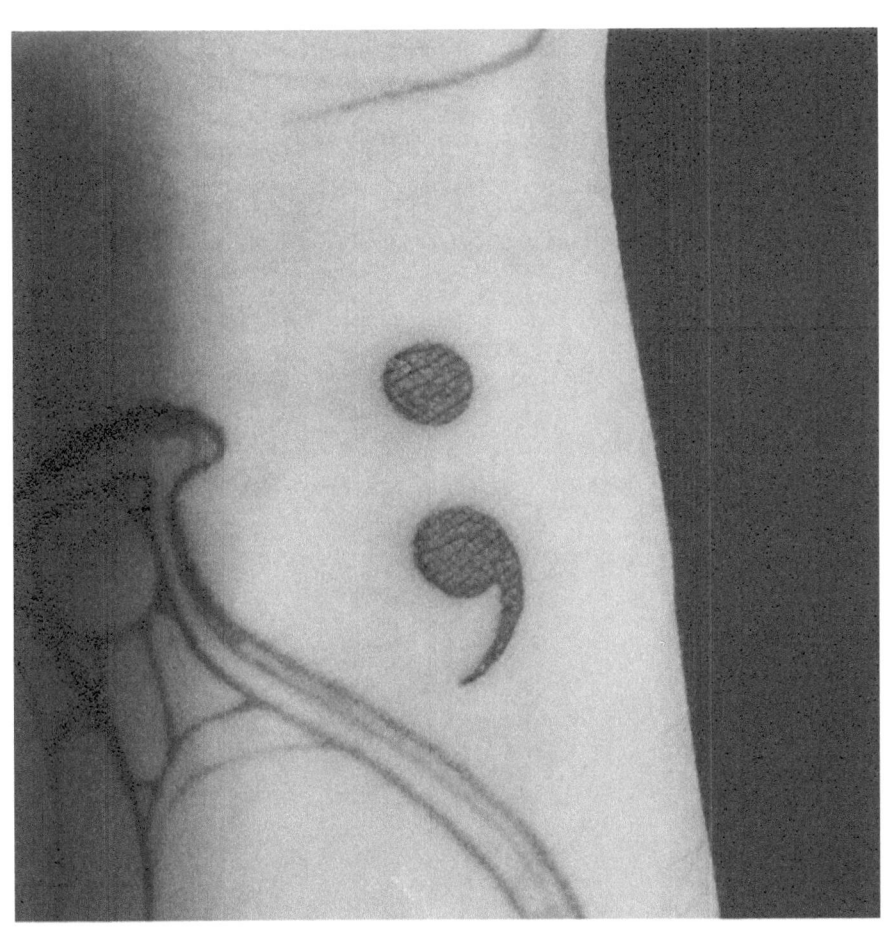

BURDEN

It's quiet.

Surrounded by the darkness.

My heavy breathing is the only sound.

I took a seat in front of the window.

Looking out at the trees.

The sound of my heartbeat was drawing in fear.

Felt less like breathing,

More like taking the breath out of me.

Wanting to be saved,

But I can't be a burden.

LAST THOUGHT

I think about you,
Every time.
Makes it harder for my hands to move,
And heavier for my heart to bear.
No matter how bad I want to,
I can feel you pull me back.

Suddenly, you remind me of that one time,
And it's like I was there again.
Remembering how happy I was,
With you again.

FAMILIAR SPACES

I never wanted to hurt anybody,
I just wanted to be heard.
Please don't cry for somebody,
That couldn't carry his words.
'Cuz look where silence got me,
I could've left my family, hurt.

ALMOST

I almost broke a promise that day,

I'm scared of what could've come next.

I almost broke a promise I made.

My thoughts nearly scared me to death.

I almost broke a promise to say,

The last words to come out of my breath.

I almost broke a promise you saved,

In hopes to close a moment I kept.

THAT NIGHT

The moon wasn't out, that night
I was scared of what came, next
There was more darkness in what was put to the light

The grip I kept on your pulse was tight
You needed more than just a text
The moon wasn't out, that night

I was scared of the thought that you might
Sometimes, it's not enough to try your best
There was more darkness in what was put to the light

I was scared to have you leave my sight
Both of our strength was put to the test
The moon wasn't out, that night

Your speech wasn't black and white
It was caught in an intoxicated mess
There was more darkness in what was put to the light

There was a moment where my heart would've said, you're right
But, we can't fall for the same hex
The moon wasn't out, that night
There was more darkness in what was put to the light

THREE BANDAGES

I put us here, in this ring.
Degrading myself into this negative corner.
Three bandages can't cover everything.

The anger in me numbed how much my fingers bled.
My coping skills went out of order.
I put us here, in this ring.

I put labels on our head we never would mean.
Couldn't cry on my own shoulder.
Three bandages can't cover everything.

Nothing felt real, like it was a dream.
Now it'll stay with me as I get older.
I put us here, in this ring.

I hurt us with my own hands in the steam.
The temp in my own thoughts was getting warmer.
Three bandages can't cover everything.

I put our blood in the stream.
I could've made our line cut shorter.
I put us here, in this ring.
Three bandages can't cover everything.

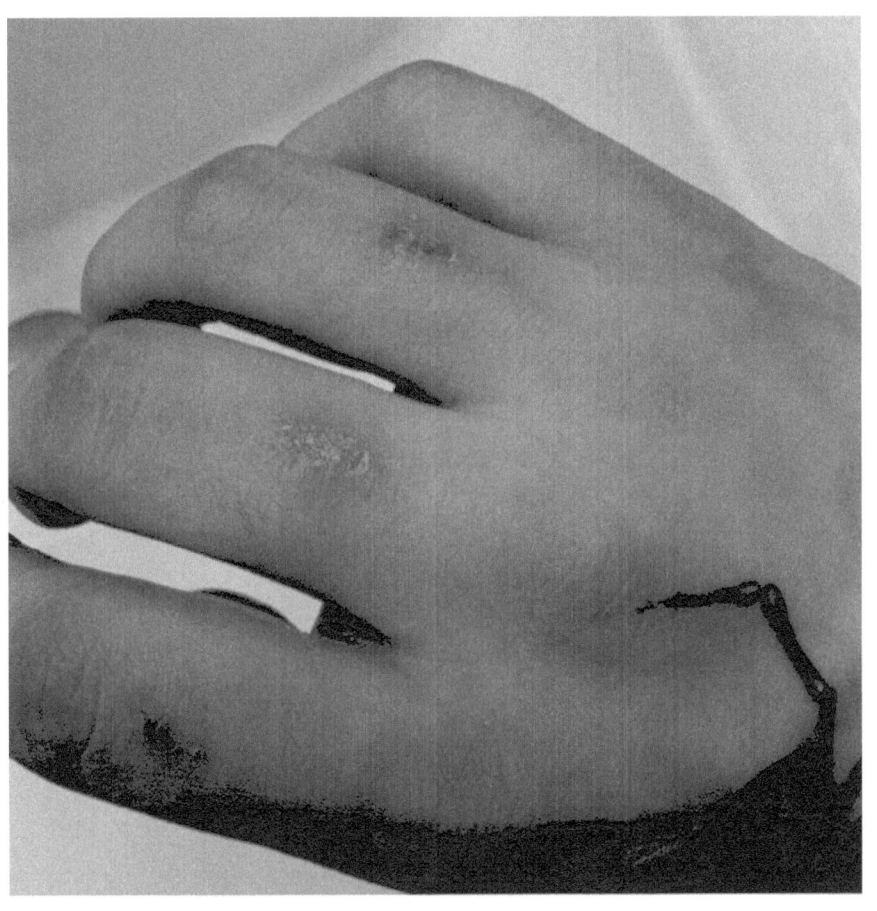

FRAGILE

I've been to my breaking point,
More times than I can count.
Not 'cuz of lack of patience,
But lack of time.

I've never said how much I could carry.
I just get a grip and keep walking.
But I can only carry so much.
Eventually, I'll break.

I've been broken before.
But I'll never let you see my scars.
'Cuz you weren't there when I stood back up,
And held the pieces of me in my hands.

Putting myself back together,
But I never looked the same after.
Something about me always changed.
Maybe I left a piece or two behind.

LESSONS

I learned to talk.
As a little boy.
You taught me that.

I learned to stay quiet.
As a young man.
You taught me that.

I couldn't tell you I wasn't okay.
I didn't know how to.

I really needed help.
But handling my problems alone,
Was what you taught me.
Was there something I missed?

FORGIVE & FORGET

He used to always forgive & forget,

But forgiving was the easy part.

'Cuz it didn't hurt anyone except himself.

Forgetting felt more like filling his pockets.

As long as he couldn't see it,

He didn't care how heavy it was to carry around.

SINKING

I fell into the deep water again.
And I couldn't call her again.
My mind wonders again,
Will I see my father again?

You remind me of my past life.
And I haven't seen him since last night.
I was dreaming of our last time,
Now, I'm missing our last time.

EVALUATE

I've loved without a purpose,
I've hurt without a cure.
I've learned what my worth is,
I've seen inside a blur.
I've accepted I'm not perfect,
I thought that I was sure.
But doing acts of service,
Doesn't mean your heart is pure.

GRIEVE

A part of me leaves,
The heart in me grieves.
It's hard to believe,
You're not in my reach.
Restarted the feed,
To tarnish the need.
We're parted and free,
Still, far from relief.

FEAR

I couldn't hold my breath,
I'd scare myself to death.
Which is ironic 'cuz,
That's all I had left.

DISCREET

I don't want to see you,
I'm afraid of your judgment.
To put labels on me,
Of someone I wasn't.

HATE

You're the strongest feeling,

Yet I'll never admit to you.

You make me burn the clothes off my skin.

You carry anger like it's light.

You're a label I never want worn by anyone.

COPE

What else can I do
When the bed is made for two?
And the trauma that I knew,
Took the place meant for you?
I didn't want to choose,
'Cuz no matter what, I lose.
On one side's an empty room,
I close my eyes and I see you.

On the other is the pressure,
Trying to keep ourselves together.
Don't want my patience used to measure
The amount of space from you, you treasure.
I'm done repeating cycles.
I'm done with changing titles.
I'm done with all the thoughts, the feelings, and memories recycled.

I'm embarrassed to be back
In this hole you left me at.
A little deeper from the past,

With more baggage to unpack.
Will the messages unfold,
All the stories that I've told?
A heart that's made of gold,
Yet, you couldn't take me home.

QUESTION

Am I someone to be proud of,

If I made it this far?

And still haven't found an answer.

To what's been haunting me.

My whole life.

PHASES

You caught my interest.

Like a bullet hitting a bulletproof vest.

It's like you were made to stop me in my tracks.

We connected on what felt like everything.

Like the final piece of a puzzle.

It's like you were made to fill in a piece of me that was missing.

We fell for each other,

Like a trust fall.

It's like we both trusted in catching each other,

Before we hit the floor.

Then, you called it quits.

Like throwing in the white flag.

You gave up on us…

LOOKING AT YOU

I don't want to put you through this again.

You don't deserve to hurt.

You don't deserve to cry.

You don't deserve to feel the way I've felt.

23

Do I deserve to be celebrated,
Why is that even a question?
'Cuz it's part of the world we created,
And birthdays are too much attention.
I'm so used to being degraded,
Every time my name is mentioned.
It hurts so much, I hate it
The spotlight came, I left it.

Presents, gifts, and messages,
From a lot of people I don't trust.
It's not about what the message is,
It's about the things that stay between us.

TRAINS

I had breakfast with a familiar face.

But it was hard for him and I to look at mine the same.

I noticed a canvas, small and seemed-to-be-finished.

But all I could notice about it was what it was missing.

Maybe I've been paying attention to the wrong things.

HIGH EXPECTATIONS

Am I high enough?
When I look down, do I fear the fall?
Or is this height in my head,
And I'm not high at all?
Am I important?
Do I get a call when I'm needed?
Or did I not really matter,
And I'm just struggling to believe it?

CLOTHES OFF

Closed off,

I'm not myself, so I took my clothes off.

Wearing a layer of shame and guilt, you couldn't hose off.

Can't run from my demons, so I dozed off.

But I see them there, too. Some things you can't just close off.

I'll keep waking up to make sure I'm alive,

'Cuz they'll always be reminders of things I've survived.

Can't run from what's inside of your mind,

If so, I'd be running blind all the time.

COME TO GRIPS

I tried to call for help,

But all that came out was tears.

I made it hard on myself,

When my thoughts made it clear.

I was ignoring my health,

Because all you brought was fear.

That's the cards I was dealt,

That's the cards that brought me here.

THE APOLOGY LETTER

I feel like we've always been in a feud, butting heads,
Could never come to an agreement, like when we started taking meds.
You were always the first to mark a mistake, at my own expense,
Always saying that I fucked up, not a consideration that it depends.
Always so easy to point the finger, 'cuz you'd never do anything wrong.
You were always so perfect, like there's no reason for this song.
Well maybe I need to say something for a change, time to take this
zipper off.
The one you put on my mouth. Like a puppet, I just went along.
Well, I'm done with it. It's because of you that I wanted to jump.
I had to take that step back. Why did I have to interrupt?
When you were supposed to protect me. Since when were we giving up?
Like that's the solution, and saying that we weren't enough?
That's not our conclusion! I am refusing that you have that control.
To do something stupid. Instead of using the support that you know.
Could stop this confusion. We are not losing! Knowing, there's someone to hold.

Our two cents. We're not a nuisance to the ones that love us the most.
But I can't be mad at you. You've been carrying our baggage for a while,
And asking for nothing back. Just giving a wave and a smile.
Like it was nothing, you've been strong for so many miles.
And now, you're just tired. You can't just keep walking in denial.
Like, your feelings are not valid. 'Cuz they matter. I'm sorry for what
we went through.
I'm sorry for blaming us for things that we didn't do.
I'm sorry for keeping us up at night. Medication helps, I always knew.
Just was always scared to take it. That decision was difficult.
We accept change. But hesitate when it's drastic.
Especially when it reminds us of things Dad did.
We have trauma. But, we're going to work through it. Together.
And we're not alone. We have love and support, whenever.

I love you, for you!

GETTING BETTER

I hope you know that I'll be okay.

I'm working on believing it too.

And I'm not just saying it to get you off my back.

I'm saying it cuz I'm doing it for me.

I thought I was done, trying to please you.

But I guess it wasn't the whole truth.

I never wanted to lie to anyone,

But I forgot to check on what I was telling myself too.

PEACE OF MIND

White nails and grey lines,
Dark tales with my rhymes.
I might fail, but I'm fine,
There's no hail in my mind.

CHECKING IN

How's your night been?

I hope you enjoyed your day.

I hope you had a good time with your friends,

I'm sorry for the choices I made.

I never meant to scare you,

There's just a lot in my brain.

I hope you're not being hard on yourself,

'Cuz Jason isn't your name.

PRIVILIGES

Missing you right now,

Keeps me wandering around my world of a mind.

Holding your hand,

Guiding us through the memories we've made so far

Eases the reality,

Knowing you're actually not next to me right now.

Our memories are a privilege,

Images and core memories that I'm grateful to be feeling pain and love for.

I LOVE YOU

You won't notice it yet,

But you had to grow up sooner than most.

You'll blame Mom and Dad,

And struggle to understand the things you did to cope.

You won't talk about it,

But you'll be there for the ones that wear your pain alone.

They'll look to you for comfort,

You'll choose to make their pain your own.

It hurts for a while,

But it's stories of pain you never told.

I love you for that,

I love you for the weight you choose to hold.

I love you for you,

I love you for the things that only me and you know.

RECOVER

GIFTED

I was told I was given a gift,

I'm still learning to use it.

I fear someday it will go to waste,

How do I not prepare for that possibility?

Putting my eggs in one basket.

Having the confidence to ultimately choose me.

NOT YET

To say I was content with lying next to you forever,
Was a broken soul looking down at his bed.
Not deserving of the comfort from its warmth
That'd keep him in his loved ones' hearts, eternally.

THANK YOU FOR SAVING ME

I've admired the sky and its clouds a little more lately.

Your smile gets me emotional.

'Cuz at one point, I thought I'd seen it for the last time.

The late-night drives feel less like I'm running away from something.

And more like I'm just driving.

Spending time alone doesn't feel like a punishment.

It's peaceful.

My thoughts haven't fully come around to change.

Nothing's perfect,

But I'm okay with it.

I've accepted that it takes time to change.

To heal.

To grow.

BECAUSE OF YOU

Hey Momma,

I enjoyed spending time with you these last couple of days.

I'm sorry for the news I gave.

I never meant to hurt you.

I never meant to make you feel like you didn't do your job right, raising me.

None of this is your fault.

I've just had a lot that I've carried inside for so long.

Eventually, it all fell on me.

Didn't think I'd get back up from the mess I made.

But, I did.

And I have you to thank for it.

I love you.

And I'm alive because of you.

TO TAKE AWAY

I was willing to die,
Knowing I was going to take this moment away.
I'll never show you how apologetic I am about it.
So instead, I'll make this moment last.
I'll show you the smile you know.
I'll laugh with you.
I'll be here with you.

And when the moment ends,
And I get in my car and start driving home.
I'm going to think about that moment,
Where I almost took away your smiles and laughs,
And made them tears and heartbreak.
And I'm going to live in that world,
As a punishment for the hurt that I almost caused,
Until I come home and learn to forgive myself.

LINE IN THE SAND

Powerless. Useless. Less Than. A Disappointment. Nobody. A Mistake.

That was a line in the sand you made in my mind.
I didn't realize that it stayed there.
I didn't realize that it never left.
I've never tried crossing it.
'Cuz those were your words.
They meant something to me.
They meant everything to me.

YOU'LL SEE

Don't let his words make you rethink your feelings.
What you went through was real.
You didn't deserve those words.
You didn't deserve those labels.

He didn't feel the pressure.
He didn't see the issues.
He didn't have a fractured rib.
He didn't try his best, only to lose.

You are not a disappointment.
You are not a mistake.
You are not a problem.
You are not a failure.

You'll see.

PRESSURE

I've felt the pressure of being human.

Now I'm home to get better.

Now there's pressure of getting better.

It never ends.

REAL GAINS

I've pulled weight, in hopes to be strong enough to carry your pain and mine.

Growing the muscle to feel the idea of being enough.

Trying to gain strength in being proud of my reflection.

It doesn't make a difference.

I still struggle to push myself together.

I still struggle to hold the pressure.

I still struggle to carry the burden.

SPILL

I opened up when I couldn't close off,

Thought I was stable till I let the rose fall.

Couldn't catch a break, not even a close call,

I'm done reaching your expectations; they're always so tall.

I've grown tired of the same advice,

Chance is, I gave more than twice.

I managed to roll the dice,

But that came with a hefty price.

STOP

Don't neglect the things that you need to say.
It matters.
You matter.
That much has been proven.

LISTEN!

There's never enough distractions to fill your void.

You have to let go!

PROGRESS

With each step forward,
A piece gets left behind.
I don't know what I'm heading toward
It's just an idea in my mind.
I can't look back at the torture shed;
They carry words that always remind
About the times that I've been cornered
By the voices that I let decide.

PATIENCE

Only time will tell on the things that have been kept behind a sealed mouth.

Every question left unanswered.

Every expression we questioned in our heads.

Every thought that wasn't expressed.

Every goodbye that's felt permanent lately.

Every... everything.

Patience is the key to those doors.

It's almost universal.

One thing it isn't is easy to come by.

It's grown through time.

It's built from what's tested its walls.

And taught by the worst mistakes.

Let time tell.

WHITE OUT

Filling spaces over your voice,
Covering the loudest noise.
This time, it is my choice,
To choose the things that I destroy.

SCREAM

I'll scream all the words,

But I'm not sure if you'll listen.

I've prepared for the worst,

To keep it out of my system.

In this lesson, I learned

To let go of things that I'm missing.

And now the time is heard

It's time to follow the wisdom.

ZIPPER

I promised I would fix you,
But that isn't what love is.
You put my words in your pocket,
And would throw them at me.
I've carried your pain more than the bags on my eyes,
I could blame it on the lack of sleep,
But our calls at night didn't help that either.

Staying awake for you,
Taking the blame for you.
Giving my time to you,
Pushing away everyone for you.

Holding back from how I felt for you.

A part of me still feels like I let you down.
Whenever I think about our moment.
I'm sorry for everything I did.
I'm sorry for everything I didn't.

I'm sorry for the zipper I kept on my mouth.

COME BACK

It's easy to hide behind a good day,

Not showing where your mind has been stranded.

Being reminded of what you are missing out on.

Remembering how to smile again.

Don't lose yourself for too long.

They've been waiting for you to find your way back.

And you don't deserve to hide the best version of yourself.

It's harsh to hug and hold a cold heart that's struggling to beat.

A THOUGHT

The truth is still,

Running loose at will.

Couldn't choose to fill,

This entire booth with real.

Never lose or kill,

I only cruise and chill.

Whatever's bruised will heal.

I'm in a ruse with feel.

FEELING FEELINGS

I couldn't keep my feelings on paper
Just the words.
I wrote till I was speechless.
Every feeling remained instilled in my prison of a human shell,
Hoping for a way out that doesn't involve showing who you don't
want to be.
The calm didn't come before the storm.
It came out, along with the last loud exhale.
It shared a spot in the rubble, with guilt
Sharing smiles that were holding back tears.
Who did I have to be in order to feel at peace?

TURN BACK

If I could turn back the time,

I'd go back to when the roses were vibrant.

To when you made the loudest voice silent.

To when the smile on my face, I couldn't hide it,

Hide the fact that I'm in love with you.

The fact that you shone on the rose in my chest and made it bloom.

The fact that you made me believe in the idea of soon.

In the darkest places, your smile shines bright as the moon.

If I could turn back the time,

I'd go back to when I first made you laugh.

To the first movie date we had.

To the first time watching you leave me, made me sad.

I'm grieving the time we have left.

DRIVING

I've been cruising on down this lone road,

Running away from places I won't go.

Trying not to stand still, giving time to those ghosts,

Hoping that no one is around to hold close.

I just keep driving. Just driving…

BREATHE

I don't have the lungs to run away from you,
You'll always catch up to me eventually.
To remind me that I'll always lose to you,
I'm just not fast enough.
If I'm already breathless,
You'd pull my lungs out of my mouth.
And leave me on the floor,
Struggling to find the air that surrounds me.
Panic. Panic. Panic.

Nobody's going to save me,
Not from you.
You know how to make me feel weak,
I just sink to the floor.
Until I can't see you no more.
And when I find myself again,
I'll take a step.
Then the next steps,
Until I see you again in the distance.
Breathe. Breathe. Breathe.

STILL BREATHING

I've judged you, in the times I've hated you.
I've degraded you 'cuz everyone else would.
I've watched you cry to see how ugly you are.
Yet, I still wiped your tears away.

I still cleaned you up when you felt dirty.
I still gave you compliments on our good days.
I guess I need to give you more credit than I have.
I've seen you at your worst.
Somehow, you're still in front of me.
Still breathing.

IT'S FAMILIAR

I couldn't be the one.

To fill a void with the sun.

I see the light and run.

Chasing after what's been done.

LONELY

It's been a couple days, since I last seen the moon

Even on my worst days

I could at least count on it to be there for guidance, back home

Lately, it's been clouds and stars in the late night

Been searching, while on my walks

I look just as lost as the lack of light makes me feel

Where did you go?

If I can't count on you to be there, every night

What does that have to say about the people you've accompanied?

PROCESSING

I don't wanna be lonely no more.

I don't wanna hold onto a memory.

I don't wanna pick my heart off the floor.

I don't wanna have to tell you to remember me.

I don't wanna carry guilt in my core.

I don't wanna keep what December brings.

I'd rather store what's left in a drawer.

I'd rather move on to better things.

DAMAGED GOODS

I've been damaged goods to the people who needed me, most

How could you depend on someone who's still working on keeping themselves together?

That kinda scares me.

'Cuz I don't want to let you down

KARMA

I've admitted to the times I've lied.

Still, I don't understand why you don't believe me when I'm not.

I guess that's just karma for lying to begin with.

But I'm concerned, why nothing has happened yet to you for your lies?

Is karma being just as unfair as life can be?

Or maybe, there's something bigger for you.

Waiting for that moment of relief.

To drag the scale back to a heavy toll.

An uphill battle.

Growing.

STAY

Begging forgiveness to make you stay.

Pleading my case to make you stay.

Wasting my tears to make you stay.

Keeping faith that you would stay.

Staying in hopes you would stay, too.

NOT MY VALENTINE

This is not the same person I met,
I look at you, and I see a façade.
You are not my best friend.
I haven't seen her since she left
You make home feel familiar,
In the way I felt when I was closed off from my own parents,
While living under the same roof.
That kind of familiarity carries a grudge,
One that I never wanted my own home to feel.

I can't trust you...

NOT GOING TO

I'm not going to beg you to stay,
I'm not going to text you first.
I'm not going to be fake,
I'm not going to claim you were the worst.
I'm not going to ignore the stain,
That you left all on my shirt.
But I got all of this pain,
What do I do when it hurts?

It comes and goes in the waves,
Like the thoughts that I saved.
When my heart can feel safe,
You come rocking my grave.
Thought I died in your brain,
Left behind in the rain.
Tried to hide in a cave,
Keeping dry from your name.

Now, my walls are just stained with the moments.
Reminders of the memories I hold in.

The times when I was heard when not a word was spoken,
I carry 'cuz I tend to mistake it for what hope is.

Someday, I will be fine, and that's all that is true.
Through this stage of life, I will keep on walking with the moon.
I will look at every light, and let it guide me to what's new.
Leave the stress I have behind, even if it involves you.

CHOOSING

Choose to be happy.
Choose to take the next step.

To be happy is to be in the moment.
To be sad is to be out of body.
To be hurt is to want protection.
To move on is to take the next step.

TO LOSE

Can't cross the line in attachment,
I'm afraid of looking you in the eyes.
I sense that I'll lose myself in them again.
Are you worth repeating the same scene?

Can I accept you as temporary is the question.
Coming and going, like waves of emotions.
You drown me in my own,
Then comfort me with yours.

I'll love you without questioning,
Knowing where this is going to go.
Even though this feeling is strong,
I'm learning to lose you.

GROWTH

I've loved, and I've loved a little more.
I've given with no objection of giving toward.
And you've taken every tear I've ever poured.
I often questioned which parts of me that you adored.

In the times I felt like I needed
Someone to love me when I was grieving,
When everyone else was up and leaving
Why was I the only one able to treat it?

Loving myself enough to heal.
Loving myself enough to be my own bandage to peel.
Loving myself enough to show my scars and reveal
The monster living inside of me is real.

HEALING

COMFORT

I remember this.

It's going to be okay.

Look how far we've come.

MOMENT

I'm in a new moment.

Pain became peace.

Loss became a new form of love.

Distance became space.

You became a moment.

STILL ALIVE

In every possible outcome,

I struggled to have a picture for this one.

'Cuz it wasn't the best-case scenario,

At first, anyway.

Now that I'm here,

Now that the storm has passed.

The rain has poured everything it had on me,

Dripping in all my grief.

Soaked through the clothes,

Feeling the uncomfortable, cold, and wet clothes sticking on and off my skin.

Nothing could dry this off

I could only keep stepping forward.

Eventually, when you continue to move forward,

You lose sight of where you were and what you were feeling.

My clothes have since dried off.

I've learned to feel comfortable and stronger in my own skin again.

Maybe this path was the best-case scenario.

After all,

I'm still alive.

INSTRUCTION

What is recovery, without reflection?
What is growth, without failure?
What is help, without attention?
What is crisis, without a savior?

Soon the answer will deprive the tension
And the choices that gave me, her
There's a cause to depression
And effect to our behavior

To recover, is to reflect
To grow, is to fail
You can't help and neglect
The same breath, you inhaled

I did wrong to expect
An unfinished boat to sail
My words were only meant
To give the idea of a trail

ROSES

I found this rose in the same field where I left my heart.

I took it with me and left my heart to grow,

Hoping it would blossom as another rose.

Time told me that this rose wasn't meant to keep its vibrant shape forever.

Eventually, it finds the floor to reach for.

So, I returned to the field of roses in hopes to see my heart thrive.

My heart saw the same fate,

Darkened, defeated, and alone.

Why did I trust you to have my heart?

FEELS LIKE HOME

Being familiar with a space that once carried two heartbeats

Has since carried a heavy dread to replace that pulse.

The shadows in the home seem darker than usual.

Her presence took a lot of the light with her.

Eventually, you learn to remind yourself that there was a feeling of home without her, once before.

How do I revert to that?

Change.

Reorganize the home,

Reclaim and redefine what was lost.

Seeing the loss as a gain.

Enjoy being home alone.

Soon enough, it feels like home.

Once more.

THE TRUTH

The truth is,

I'm nothing special.

I'm no different from everyone else.

I don't know who you are,

But at one point, I thought you were just like me.

I know now that that isn't true.

I'm learning to be okay with that,

Not because I wish it was true,

But because I used to think it was the truth.

TIME

I took the time I needed to grieve.

To process the amount of time you took in my life,

While trying not to overthink about the time you left me to get back up.

It's almost disrespectful. Yet, I know it's not your intent.

It's not like you to hurt me.

Maybe I'm just trying to convince myself on that last point.

GRIEVING

Love is gone.

Grief is here.

My heart is strong.

It's hard to appear.

Rewrite my wrongs,

Can't erase what won't clear.

I've held this bond,

The only time I hold fear.

THE START AND THE FINISH

I couldn't see the signs from behind your eyes.
I could only see myself and the way you made me smile.
Blinded by your shine, I didn't mind the darkness.
I could only feel your love, even with my eyes closed.

I'm still seen when my presence isn't felt.
I'm still heard when I haven't said a word.
I was blinded by your understanding.
I didn't notice the finish line, till it was too late.

YOU DON'T UNDERSTAND

I want you to leave
The pictures of us.
Your scent on my clothes.
Our favorite places.
Your things in my home.
The memories we made.
The lessons you taught.
The moments I stay in.
My heart that you took.

YOU STILL GET TO ME

If I'm the problem, how do I become the answer?

If you won't give me a route, I'll make me a path

Just to show you I'm trying. Proving a point

I'm not supposed to prove anything to you. So why do I continue?

Why does your opinion of me, matter so much to try to change?

I thought I let go of you, already. Somehow you still linger

Somehow, I still miss you. You still get to me

EVERY THIRTY MINUTES

Every five years, I don't know where I'm going to be.

Every year, I'm hoping to see it.

Every couple of months, I don't have a plan for.

Every couple of weeks, I could maybe make an idea of it.

Every week goes by fast.

Every couple days, I'm hoping for the best.

Every day, I try to make the most of it.

Every couple of hours, I try to accomplish something.

Every hour, I might write another poem.

Every thirty minutes, I try not to overthink.

Every thirty minutes, I try not to listen to the voices.

Every thirty minutes, I focus on my breathing.

Every thirty minutes is how I go through life.

I GUESS SOME THINGS, I'LL NEVER KNOW

I guess some things, I'll never know

Do you still think about me?

Would you still mourn me when that day comes?

Am I something to you, I'll never be?

I guess some things, I'll never know

I'm still learning how to let you go

'Cuz you used to be the only home I know.

When I'm gone, do the memories show?

I guess some things, I'll never know

WILL YOU CATCH ME?

If I fall, will you catch me?

This leap of faith in the next step.

If I close my eyes and step forward

If I fly toward the ground, without my wings,

Chasing only an idea of what could be,

With only faith in my hands and an answer at the bottom

Will you catch me?

BELIEVING IN MYSELF

I'm going to be okay.

It's about time I have faith in that.

It's about time I start to believe in it.

Letting go of everything that hurts to carry.

Enjoying, taking the lighter steps in life.

Enjoying life without the idea of you.

Without the constant "What Ifs" in mind.

Putting myself first.

ACCEPTING CHOICES

Taking chances.

Betting on love.

Dying on this hill.

Standing on my decision.

No matter what happens.

I'm grateful for it.

Every smile, every trial.

No matter the pain.

No matter how alone I felt.

I needed it.

And I'm better now because of it

JUST WANTED TO TELL YOU

How do I tell you, I'm thinking of you?

Do I write you a letter?

Do I like your post?

Should I send you a message?

Should I call your phone?

Should I carve your name in the stars?

Should I whisper your words in the wind?

Should I pray for a sign?

Even if I don't believe?

Maybe you'd already know if I just left you alone.

LABELS

A new face.
A new friend.
Someone I trust.
My best friend.
My greatest fear.
The biggest heart.
Misunderstood.
Another reason.
My love.
My every thought.
A void in the room.
Just a roommate.
My secret.
A liar.
My pain.
A gas to the flame.
A fresh restart.
A friend.
A sudden stop.

A brick wall.
A blocked contact.
A reopened cut.
A loss.
My last teardrop.
Just another moment.
My dead rose.

NOT ANYMORE

I don't think about you as often anymore
You made that easy for me
I'm grateful you made that hard decision
'Cuz I know I wouldn't have the strength in me to pull that trigger
Loving you from a distance
Is still loving you
All that's left is time
To tell me what to do with it

I don't think about you as often anymore
Only pieces of our moment that felt like another life
A dream that felt too real, at one point
Then the bad news came and woke me up
Maybe the bad news was I woke up
Now, I just remember
And it continues until I remind myself of where I am
Part of me hopes you struggle with the same thing
But most of the time, I just hope you're okay
I hope that you're happy
I hope you're better off without me

THIS CANDLE

This candle has been lit.

It's wandered through the heaviest storms,

The harshest winds.

It's walked through the rain without an umbrella.

Hell, it's even withstood being spat at, out of spite.

Yet, it's always kept its flame throughout it all.

You'd expect that flame to have turned to smoke at an accidental sigh.

The flame only grew.

It could've started fires,

Made the sky turn black,

Let it rain the ashes of its own sparks,

Made a difference in the world around it.

Eventually, it did make a difference

But not in the way expected.

This candle wandered around its world, alone.

A world that needed a light to guide a heartbeat.

The candle became that light for the people around it.

No matter the destination or journey.

And with every person it crossed paths with, or guided,

It left them with a spark

Strong enough for them to light a candle themselves,

And become a light.

The candle wasn't worried about losing its flame with how much it was giving.

Its only worry was not giving enough.

And every new spark made that candle question if it was enough.
But it never stopped in its tracks to think about it.
It just kept moving forward.
If only it had stopped and taken a look back at where it came from,
It would've seen the lit path behind it
Candle after candle, bringing light to a dark world,
While it roamed, questioning every second of its existence
If it was enough to make a difference.

GRATEFUL

I always felt the safest with you.

You never judged the things I said.

You just let the ink spill.

Arguably the greatest listener.

The times when I closed you off.

You would wait till I came back, to welcome me with a warm embrace.

I've told you my secrets.

I've told you my deepest thoughts.

I'm grateful,

'Cuz you saved my life.

WHEN I THINK OF YOU

When I think of you,

I won't think of the times when it was hard to be in the same room.

I'll think about the times when we couldn't stay away from each other.

I won't think about the times you pushed me away.

I'll think about the times when you held me close.

I won't think about the times you made your love disappear.

I'll think about the times when you couldn't hide your love, if you tried.

I love you enough to always remind you that I do.

And I'm learning to love you enough to let you go.

WHAT'S LEFT

I couldn't leave what was left of you, on paper

So, I left it on a record, to play when I get lonely

Songs that reek of dead roses and smeared hearts

And a voice of a soul that believed in a promise

Maybe it's too late now for wasting our breath

But it would've made me think you cared, if you would tell me

I'm bad for you because love became an addiction to cover the truth

left, unsaid

And the words 'love' and 'lies' got stuck in a grey area inside our minds,

too blurry to tell apart

I don't carry wishes cuz they take up too much space

But I still read them from the safe, I put them in

Wishing for a fresh start

Wishing for understanding

Wishing to read your mind

A recipe for clarity and closure that I'll never get...

GOODBYE

I'm not saying goodbye to what I know
I'm saying goodbye to what I knew
Goodbye to the plans, made
Goodbye to the beginning of something, special
Goodbye to what could've been

THE END

We sat here alone,

I was scared to see the difference.

Who once felt like home,

Has closed off every entrance.

Lately, it's been cold,

I don't blame it on being Christmas.

Ever since you have been gone,

It's felt like more than distance.

Between us. My demons have reasons to see us. Do you understand?

I needed to breathe in, to keep in this feeling; it's out of my hands.

It's all on my shoulders. I'm holding composure and a handful of strands.

I loved you, not judged you. I want to not want you. I don't know if I can.

3I can't shake it. Won't fake it. My heart was mistaken.

I'm patient. I hate it, 'cuz I thought that we made it.

Just aimed at my statements and shot back the claims that

I made in the pages. So, it's over. New stages.

It's hard for me to accept. So, I guess I'll keep it in.

Pretending that I'm fine.

Like, it's okay to be your friend.

I won't forget that smile and the words that you had meant.

You left me at my lowest. Safe to say that it's the end.

I COULD BE LONELY

I'm learning a familiar lesson.

Not the kind of lesson you learn at a desk.

The kind you learn by walking down a lonely road.

The kind you learn by standing still,

Sitting in a room,

Taking a drive at three in the morning.

I'm learning to be alone.

I needed you there,

For everything.

Not because I needed you to complete me,

But because I needed you to be another voice around

That's not my own.

I can scare myself, sometimes.

It's always nice to have another person who is there to catch me

Not when I fall,

But when I stumble.

I'll learn to handle myself.

I'll learn to walk this lonely road.

But, while I'm on this journey,

I got to admit

Sometimes…

I could be lonely.

MONSTERS

The monsters from under my bed,
Feel more like close friends.
Growing up is realizing that they never truly leave.
They grow up with you.
They evolve from under your bed to everywhere you go.
You might even see them in the mirror.
They become more involved in your life.
They give themselves names like
Anxiety, Guilt, Sadness, and Anger.
Feeding you things like negativity,
And are your best friend when no one's around.

They are not your friends,
Just versions you convince yourself you are.
Don't listen to them.

LETTING GO

Letting go, if it means healing,
Letting go, if it hurts less.
Letting go, if it stops bleeding,
Letting go, if it holds a mess.

Letting go of burdened weight,
Letting go of thinking the worst.
Letting go of memories we made,
Letting go of smiles that hurt.

Letting go, till I feel light,
Letting go, till I float to the surface.
Letting go, till I see the why.
Letting go, till I'm shown my purpose.

LOVE YOURSELF

I struggle to be proud of the person in the mirror,

Watching that person work on himself constantly,

Only to end every day feeling like it wasn't enough.

I used to see him find joy in working out and going to the gym.

Now, lately, he's been holding back tears in between sets.

It's like he's lost his reason behind why he does it

Or maybe his reason hasn't been the easiest to work through.

I know he notices the growth.

I just feel like he's constantly comparing himself to who he used to be,

Trying to live up to what felt like a prime moment.

I hope he eventually accepts himself for who he is,

And loves himself just as much as I do

SO, WHERE DO WE GO NOW

Forward.

Anywhere.

The next step.

I have no idea.

To go get food.

To the next chapter.

Wherever the journey takes me.

Fuck off…

THANK YOU

For the nights you stayed

For the conversations I needed

For the hugs that saved me

For the reminders of who I am

For the times you were open minded

For the patience you've had

For the endless supply of love I have

For the hard times I questioned

For the tears you caught

For the times you checked in

For the inspiration you gave

For the moments that were hard

For the memories I'll always wear

For the truth when it hurt

For the lies that time exposed

For being the reason, I am who I am

Jason

- Communication

- Honesty
- Love
- Acceptance
- Transparency

- Creating
- My friends/family
- My coworkers
- Working out
- Wearing an outfit that makes me confident

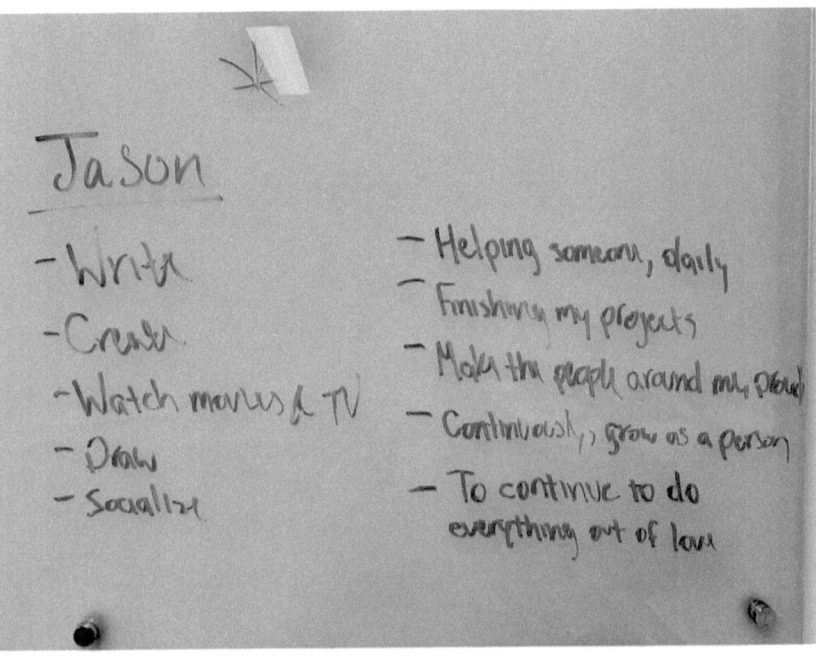

Jason

- Write
- Create
- Watch movies & TV
- Draw
- Socialize

- Helping someone, daily
- Finishing my projects
- Make the people around me proud
- Continuously grow as a person
- To continue to do everything out of love

- My importance
- My value
- My mistakes

- The little things
- My obsessions